PLAY BUTTON

Play Button

Liz Robbins

Cider Press Review, LLC
San Diego • Callifornia • USA

PLAY BUTTON

Cider Press Review, LLC
PO BOX 33384
San Diego, CA, USA
CIDERPRESSREVIEW.COM

First edition
09 9 8 7 6 5 4 3 2 1 0

ISBN: 978-1-930781-09-2
Library of Congress Control Number: 2011943224

Cover art, *Beach Stand-Off,* by Sara Pedigo.
Author photograph by Scott S. Smith.
Cover design by Caron Andregg.

ABOUT THE CIDER PRESS REVIEW BOOK AWARD:

The annual Cider Press Review Book Award offers a $1,500 prize, publication, and 25 author's copies of a book-length collection of poetry. For complete guidelines and information, visit
CIDERPRESSREVIEW.COM/BOOKAWARD.

Printed in the United States of America
at BookMobile, in Minneapolis, MN.

ACKNOWLEDGEMENTS

Many thanks to the editors of the following magazines, where some of these poems first appeared or are forthcoming:

Apalachee Review: "Love Is Changing, and I Won't Change"
Barn Owl Review: "Jesus, My Suitor"
Barrow Street: "Find a Word in Mike and Danica's Marriage"
Bayou: "Bang"
Birmingham Poetry Review: "Intuition, or Methods of Transportation"
Borderlands: Texas Poetry Review: "Orchid Room in a Botanical Garden"
Cave Wall: "Going Back" and "Poem with Oceanic Variables"
Cimarron Review: "Kentucky Derby Poem (2008)"
DMQ Review: "The Letter (1940)" and "The New Art Professor, Dead by His Own Hand"
5 A.M.: "Bronze Melting"
Greensboro Review: "Gut-Ropes"
Gulf Stream: "God Poem," "Jason Lee Wheeler's Song," and "October Tricks with the Denver Broncos"
Harpur Palate: "Poem with Bathtub, Foils"
Louisiana Literature: "Life Cycle"
MARGIE: "Bride Far Away" and "Sex Trafficker's Pantoum"
National Poetry Review: "Lucky Strikes"
New Ohio Review: "House on the Lake"
Parthenon West Review: "Horror Flicks, or Poem Beginning with a Line by Auden" and "Made-Up"
Pebble Lake Review: "Postcard Never Sent to the Black-Haired Pilot of My Former Universe"
PMS (poemmemoirstory): "The Circle"
Poet Lore: "Unwrapped"
Puerto del Sol: "Poem with Corset Allusion"
RATTLE: "Three Rivers Meet, Become Falls"
Redactions: "Our Nukes"
Saw Palm: "Postcard from an Old Lover with Picture of a Horse and Carriage, Driver and Whip"
Skidrow Penthouse: "Amy, Wanting a New Song, Imagines"
storySouth: "Partial Psychoanalytic Transcript of Christmas Day" and "Peach Dream"
Swarthmore Literary Review: "Painting with Winter Scene"
Verse Daily: "Kentucky Derby Poem (2008)"
Whiskey Island: "Sonnet from Memory"
MAYDAY Magazine: "Who's Driving"

I'm grateful to *Redactions*, especially Mike Dockins, for nominating "Our Nukes" for the Pushcart Prize, and to Erin Belieu for naming "God Poem" a finalist for *Best of the Net, 2010* (thanks to *Gulf Stream's* David Svenson for nominating).

Thanks also to the editors of Woman Made Gallery's *Her Mark: A Journal of Art and Poetry* (2009) for selecting "An American Artist Marries" for inclusion.

Many thanks to the following groups and individuals who helped make the poems happen: Kim Bradley, Jay Hopler, Sonja Livingston, Laura Lee Smith, the Flagler College Department of English, the Flagler College Administration, and my students.

A heartfelt thank you to William S. Robbins, in memoriam.

Special thanks also to Sara Pedigo for the use of her painting, *Beach Stand-Off*.

Special thanks to Caron Andregg, Ruth Foley, and Robert Wynne for their good and generous work. And to Patricia Smith, for pushing "Play."

For the renewable light and energy sources:
my mother and father, Susannah Savery, and DMR

CONTENTS

POEM WITH OCEANIC VARIABLES

Equations. What Jane, Suki, and I were
supposed to be studying, Algebra
on a Saturday evening. Instead,

Juno's Drive-Thru for two six-
packs and no I.D.
Twelve divides three times into

forgetting. The real work and sorrow,
bloodied on the road
a year or two ahead.

The night tattooed with telephone poles,
palm trees, pink buzz
of bar signs. Jane's car, a dark safety,

double bed we'd curl up in, planning
our slip into the
adult world. Solitaire black-eyed

sailors crouched on bar stools, waiting.
Lit smokes, cherry beacons.
The whole weekend turning

to three-day growth on pirated islands.
The wind, the wind, the wind
nudging, There. Yes.

At the smell of the sea pulling back.

JESUS, MY SUITOR

took me to The Fair, our long hair set
free by Ferris Wheel wind, and he shot
ducks dead in a tub of water. Almost won me
a black rubber snake. I wore a shrunken
dress of lace and shiny Mary Janes, I was one
of those groupie types pissed about a lot
of things, my hand on his jeans
in The Tunnel of Love. Jesus carried
in his jacket a flask of red wine. What else
could've been the genesis
of madness, I couldn't unwind
what people knew about me or wanted to.
We rode bumper cars, banged
my eyes shut each time we hit. Nudged
close for overturns, the swinging
pirate ship. Drove me home
in his gold Corvette, O, revved chariot
of hard rock and a quiet place.
Above, comprehensive limbs, dry
leaves. Our mouths candy-apple wine sticky.
When Jesus kissed me, he used his tongue
to pass on what may've been a slip
of qualms in code. He never called again.
For forty nights, I bowed to the dream of
my bedroom window before he pressed
the bell, front porch altar lit with him cradling
his nose in the head of a raw, clipped rose.
Gently, so as not to prick his palms.

WASTED LAMENT

The wrong kind of girl, she wanted the wrong kind
of men. Like most bad girls, she was divorced

from reality. Inside, she was good; that's how she thought
people saw her. Inside, a child, listening to her mother

read Little Red, unable to see the wolf
in that mirror. She craved velvet cake, unwilling to pick

green cabbage. Bearded men, sliding back on the mattress.

In her hands, the perpetual draft
beer, cigarettes, low cards drawn at poker. Her uniform:

red lipstick, hoop earrings, short black skirt flipping
in the breeze—too much she was

unclean, sinking, attracting the base. The frat
boys' hypothesis proved: girls who wore hoops and smoked

were easy. Five o'clock shadow guys rolling from bed
to eye the last sun's glint on her sink's dirty cups.

Like poker chips, her family flipped, friends
scattered. Love came, but in tiny slips, the fluttering insides

of fortune cookies. O, how hardly she forgets the twenty
ways she folded.

KENTUCKY DERBY POEM (2008)

Eight Belles, the filly who snapped
her ankles—had to be euthanized right
on track—
is not unlike the girl
in Moldova who leapt from five stories
to flee sex traffickers who'd stolen her.

Except the girl snapped her back, too.
Got carted to Emergency so alive
she was green bruised, red cut, begging for
more drugs.

The horse, said the news, had endured
excessive whipping.

The girl, too, of a kind.

To go back, to press on, changes nothing.

Mint in glasses, fat flowers on hats.
Horses beneath keepers, watching
for cues, waiting to move.

The girl in bed, as before. Legs hoisted
by contraptions. Doctors hovering
like captors, telling her
to lie still. They do not ask how

this happened. She dreams
of permanent escape like
the old dream of love.

The lush betting crowd cheers.
Doctors snap on rubber.

The empowered world, hiding
its hands in gloves.

POEM WITH BATHTUB, FOILS

after Berryman

1.

At what point did shifts occur? Did the mirrored
face make cliffs of fractal rock? She, about
to leave thirty-six, yet November's fall
back—that extra hour—more than she can do.
Her house's rooms—blankets, clocks,
books, fur, carpets—are some of what she loves,
despises, they are so much her. The little white
dog comes and goes, lies down, sighing. Out
the window, wind moves the rain tree, sheds
the skin-colored blooms. She starts a bath, waits
on the bed, the water going like a promise, she
cannot stand to smell her hands, her hair,
her mind, twisting from the night, the still-
blue-ing dreams.

2.

What so bad, at thirty-six? Only the relative
few dead, not yet the Do Not Go Gently, nor
the As I Lay Dying. The sun has not yet
run, her husband whistles, digs shallow,
plants marigolds in ground.

3.

She tried so long to mum. To speak would
be risk, she sensed accurately. But felt the poke
of pride and change, a painter's smock she'd
admired in a shop so bought, though the sleeves
too wide, pockets worn. Such a bright green like
the sprawled lawn of the Castillo de San Marcos,
where students sun themselves in shadows
of penetrable coquina. A bad fit, her thought
and mouth speaking. Now all the world see jade
scales, tail, teeth, fire. And saw clearly. Helplessly,
the no-defense.

4.

Emails arrive, should she open? Encoded with
(imagined?) slights and black screened. In
the evenings, the modem slaps down, but is still-
darkened connection. She has friends somehow,
but all the unsent missives go
like valentines to June, who hates her most. As
she suspects June's right.

5.

Does she offend all with her useless heart
of the personal? She tried no pride, she tried
disdainful, haughty. Now she hide.
She try all-ways, and hides what works. White
bear in a snowbound cave, thick has grown her
hide. Teeth, kept in, hidden, pornographic art.
So long, the dead arousal of sleep.

6.

At the kitchen counter, she stands before
a bowl of pretzels. One bite, and the dog
comes running: o, tiny bliss! Onto the pink
tongue to place a twist, one's heartbeat
the corresponding crunch echo! To share
becomes un-difficult within love's salty
laps! (What we shan't say: she holds all
the snacks.)

7.

When June demand her sharing, she gnarled
yellow teeth and no-love-there. And hide. *No
person ever looks miserable who feels that he
has the right to make a demand on you.* Then
she feel black soot inside. Make June yellow
cheese sandwich equivalent. Feel weak. The bee
sting, make honey, die.

8.

"I wait for Joe to come home, so I can toast
bread, melt cheese, pop soda. He's out tossing
a plastic disc far across a field. He say, You
don't need make food, woman! I, a grown
man! But my feet root to floor. Duty burn.
I, with cellophane wrap, bound. Foiled. I put out.
The plate, Joe. You don't have to, he means.
He and I know I don't
do."

9.

She got no baby, babyfies her dog. Kisses
it dead on the mouth. Who's mommy's sweet
bunny, she cries, confused. Good thing it don't
speak human. Like a god,
the dog gets all needs met. And without
a spoken word. Not the burlap sacks and straps
to the back, but the monks got right howls
of silence. Too late to make herself
right?

10.

Three impossible tasks, say Freud. To teach,
govern, cure. She mutters this in hot
baths. Epsom salts for nerves. There's reasons,
see, can't teach nobody. No dog, no June, no
god, no he. Why drive shudders to a stop. No
good. No bath for what she got.

REST, VANESSA

As if she'd been paid to stroke
my hair with the punishing brush,
ironing into tight tails, breath on
the nape. After, Vanessa
babysitter wore down the sole
of a violet boot, gas pedal felled
on the way to Salem
packs. Lucky, my diary on the dash
smelling of powder, the ABBA
8-track going, but the windshield,
her vanity television, somewhere
a play button:
Here, the field where Kenny
swung his tongue into her neck's
diamond hollow. This eatery,
she lifted a mug of tea
to his forked French toast. Sperm
designs cut into the boots, she
resorting to the usual Sassoon
jeans backbend gold thread
stitched on ass pockets. Which
had nothing to do with sex
exactly, but that Kenny smelled
blue, and Vanessa had been
practicing, pulling him up
from the longing yellow grass
with both hands, so they might
laugh, he might swish dirt from
her rumored back. Then she
could whisper it for her
mind as she turned up degrees,
the chocolate chip cookies always
going to ash.

HIGHWAY OF DISBUDDED HORNS

I've never been to
purgatory, but I plan to
keep going till I find the
part most like a Nashville
trailer park. Where virtue
is a glass of sudsy beer, a
drooped laundry line. I'll
drive slowly past the smoke
mouths, holes in dirt
mounds run riot with blue
forget-me-nots. Here where
news is a fishy river, I'll strip
my fringe jacket, swim in
fingers and eyes spread
between blinds. I'll ricochet
among wood doors as I did
all my life, soliciting a kind
of country song. Boys
hawking chocolate Santas;
girls, mascara to darken
windows. But I won't
leave till my red pickup
bed is loaded with goats.
For I have yet to arrive
at a destination
unsmeared by bleating.

SONNET FROM MEMORY

in memory of Lauren

You made the headlines—U.S. Magistrate's
Daughter Killed in I-95 Wreck—
your father still ruling over you, your fate,
his title, bold above your broken neck.
So I remember your car's ashtray, filled
with potpourri to disguise your habit
from him, the smell of your persistent will,
dead rose petals and Marlboro Reds mixed.
In the bright parlor, effusive bouquets,
the coffin plumped with silk, your mother's face,
crumpled, thin as dust from a cloisonné
urn on a shelf; here, the faintest trace
of how you drove yourself, headstrong and fast,
the lingering scent of flowers and ash.

HORROR FLICKS, OR POEM BEGINNING WITH A LINE BY AUDEN

About suffering, they were never wrong, the
cold bastards. A man with his dead mother
in a rocker plus a nicknamed
dagger always equals a woman
crying in the shower. Or a crazy lady
talking to herself in the kitchen, chopping
off heads of cabbage. Which is where
cheap beer comes from. Adulthood's a shrinking
and enlarging of pupils: the unmasked
brute tiptoeing in the bedroom, *C'est la guerre.*
The TV on Halloween doesn't care, reruns
the same scenes, your bit lip leaks
chocolate. Give it back, the hammering
heart a thumb in the mouth could still!
The irises are tired. The half-naked girl goes
screaming across a barley field, so what
quiets her? God
returns for Tarantino's next picture: a guilt-
eating virus on a Harley.

MADE-UP

The waiter abandons his teepee
of breadsticks and tiny green pool
of oil. This, the fourth table
like a bed in four days. I can't
find the opening, the exported
insides of something, the melting
fish eggs I'd eat almost accidentally
and fall in love. Someone has turned
up the A/C in hopes I'll miss the
punched-in geometry of the chain-
link fence outside and past,
the murderous blue river that
dampens smokestack dreams.
Fine, there's no smeared picture
and no gun in my purse, no
soundtrack going featuring
Greg's knees as my vodka
climaxes into the bowl. I'm running
out of things to hold
dear, which explains the shadows
above my eyes, the nails gone
vicious, the wine bored at its
window, the mad candelabra:
I've known forever the uptight
chair across from me, covered
in hysterical plaid, a left coat.

SEX TRAFFICKER'S PANTOUM

A woman not beaten is like a house not cleaned
in Moldova and Ukraine, Uzbekistan.
She is not the victim that she seems:
she smiles as she performs her little dance

in Moldova and Ukraine, Uzbekistan.
Her brows are plucked, she struts in painted jeans.
She smiles as she performs her little dance.
I keep her passport, now she is sixteen.

Her brows are plucked, she struts in painted jeans.
She was not gang-banged at the auto plant.
I keep her passport, now she is sixteen.
I buy her vaccines, condoms, breast implants.

She was not gang-banged at the auto plant,
but rings the help hot-lines with wicked schemes.
I buy her vaccines, condoms, breast implants.
I feed her meat and speed beyond her dreams,

she rings the help hot-lines with wicked schemes.
She is not the victim that she seems.
I feed her meat and speed beyond her dreams.
A woman not beaten is like a house not cleaned.

PACK OF LEAVES

Stephanie with the big boobs and big
hoop earrings, hair cut like a boy's.
We weren't there the night she fell
off the bridge. My sister, drinking
vodka fruit juice a good ways up
the wrong direction. We were
sitting around someone's studio
on the floor in front of the fireplace,
the fire going. Sitting around in our
underwear with Colin. Playing a
board game—no, everything locked
up, a beer game, strip quarters.
Soldier bodies trying to celebrate the
freedom fiesta. Everyone unemployed,
someone always leaving. No real
attachments—joints, passed. We didn't
know Stephanie's falling, ember-eyed.
Colin packing a menthol smoke on his
wrist. Dark room with glass
candlestick brass bowl stars, out in
the boondocks. We drank, I picked up
white chalk to make a Ouija board,
but forgot. The lone wolf operetta
of Stephanie already going. My sister,
swimming the black water. So deep
within, she couldn't be heard. I had only
without. Tasted mint, kissing Colin.

POSTCARD NEVER SENT TO THE BLACK-HAIRED PILOT OF MY FORMER UNIVERSE

Notice the solar system on the back, the *You Are Here* arrow pointing to Earth or perhaps a black hole. Where did you go? How far could you get in ripped jeans, ribbed tank, reeking of limes in gin? I heard you were in New York or L.A., or back home in Smalltown with your mom, who, when you were young, sprinkled pot in your cereal to keep you quiet. Do you own a gun? Do you still lie down with strays? How many times, a bit actor in dinner theater plays? Did you ever just settle in: o, you'd never believe how keen a small house, a good spouse can be. Long ago, you called me a dark star, and it's true. Fixed I was, constant, feebly glowing about you, which is why you'll never know I cried in a bathtub of wine and dreamed a letter complete with XXX and a number, still raising the scar. How much did I love you or myself to want to end.... I hate your lips, your eyes. Things that never moved enough, then roamed too far.

UNWRAPPED

When my friend Lauren wrapped
the hood of her car around a tree,
I was sixteen and still of the belief
love did not unstick with death
or time. I thought the memory
in my mind of her honey-streaked hair
and gravelly laugh would remain
intact, that I'd, in fact, pull it up,
turn it over like a stone daily, that
as a friend, I was obligated to.
But within days, I'd already begun
to suspect the reverse was true,
that despite what I'd learned
in Sunday School, I might not
see her again. No one would
know if I let her memory go
the way of feathered hair, roller skates,
The Bee Gees. Only now and then
remembering, feeling the same
purple twinge, only darker, as when
I'd step on an elevator, hear an airy
"How Deep Is Your Love?"
and know I'd survived the world
for years despite blissful naivete, a state
of mind I'd never recover. Why else
would I, weeping on her bed a few
days after, notice the pack of
Carefree gum on her night stand
and steal a stick? Why place it on
my tongue like a spearmint wafer,
chew it then swallow, all for the
little piece sure to stick—as I'd been
warned—forever inside?

GOD POEM

The tiny bearded king made of pixels
bounces from cloud to cloud. With x-ray
vision, he zaps tinier men wearing tweed
suits like body armor and even tinier
women, some holding close
the egg-shaped *Book of Secrets*.

You shift the joystick, try to help the men
and women dodge the king's orange rays like
deadly sunshine. But you don't feel too bad
for them: when they're not dodging rays,
they're hoarding gold chalices.

Then the purple gnome arrives, the one with
the limp and funny hat who resembles your
widowed Aunt Janine. The one you never
held a rosary for, the one who baked
without you sugar forgiveness cookies.

If you push the red button, some of the men
and women create a chair out of
their arms, carry the gnome over the bridge,
past the fire pit, and into the straw
hut that never catches fire.

The orange rays continue: more gnomes pop
up. You keep pushing the red button.
The people keep helping gnomes to safety.

Eventually the golden key appears.
The 1,000 pink bonus points flash on and
on, your heart goes up. Your hands are good
and strong, a level shifts.
Only then does the king vanish.

NO-SHOW AT THE NEXT WAKE

No wine, but water. At the big doors
powder cologne comes/goes. Whispers
into cell phones. In the adolescent garden,
someone's turned on
the fountain. Why
balloons, why blue? A girl snaps
pictures, what for? A woman
in an avian flu mask, carrying *petits fours.*

But his sister has strewn a table with stuff
from his young room,
he was
the star
wars tape camp pictures swim
trophies cards with his name. I didn't even know
it, but I heard his sister and him smiling
at me from within the picture frame, and the
heart's trapdoor just goes. Watery undergrowth
suddenly flush
with flightless birds.

HOW TO PICK A LOCK

Lock picking is easy. Start by introducing
    your dog. Look for a thread of a smile, silver
    glinting in ore.

The theory of lock picking is the theory of
    exploiting mechanical defects. Especially your
    own: the bedtime Zoloft, love of tabloids, how
    you weren't the favorite child.

Consult a catalog of traits and defects found in locks,
    learn the techniques used to recognize them.
    Inspect the well-known: the bruised mortise,
    the escapist bored-in, the needy interlocking.

Practice many times on the same lock as well as on
    different locks. Bid farewell to the ones left to
    rust: O, college crush, O, friend. Old bosses
    and God.

Lock picking is one of many ways to bypass a lock,
    though it causes less damage than brute force
    strategies. Avoid needling the tightest springs—
    or stay forever crouched in a sweat, squinting.

Apply a steady, gentle pressure. Work together on
    ends: imagine mixing a CD or wine party,
    growing tomatoes or kids.

Avoid applying too much pressure, as this can cause
    a lock to stick. Give deadbolts room to glide open.
    Stand alone on buildings at night for the floodgate
    of stars. Then turn toward whomever is home.

Your proof will be the click.

BANG

So of course we had again driven out (the devil)
to the desert, for when I woke up in
the trunk, I could see through the bullet holes
bleached skulls of cattle and tumbleweeds.
Next to me was the girl in the orange sundress
sealed in a Glad bag or maybe I was wrapped
in a blanket. Night-sky yearbook with the football
star eyes punched out. Do I taste out-of-date
pennies? Does it make me an Indian
giver, now I'd rather finger-fuck? Perhaps
why I'm missing: so I can nurse
holes the width of citrus groves. If I had a
zipper, I'd undo this part
about you taking the leather jacket
gang to Vegas with me
ice-chested in the makeshift
outhouse. Instead, I dream
to pieces: kick up the backseat, kiss
in your front teeth. In reality, I bellycrawl
out the keyhole into my usual fog, where I play
a wading pool at night, the crotch
of a go-go girl in rhinestone tights.

OUR NUKES

1. Our nukes are in the habit of hiding themselves below ground as if shy, much like what the proverbial ostrich does with her head. Nukes from other countries reportedly do this too, sometimes hiding so superhumanly well as to have turned invisible. Do nukes work better as rumor than fact?

2. Our nukes resemble supermodels: tall and slender, with shiny designer garb and bared teeth. They saunter expertly, capable of overriding strong reverberations of hunger. They're up on current wartime factions.

3. A woman in Detroit who screws together nuke parts says she'd rather make garbage disposals.

4. Our nukes are necessary demonstration, like good manners. We gladly pay 450 billion for a single year's etiquette lesson. A woman in Kaesong dreams our nukes wearing diapers. A father in Brooklyn whose son dissolved like a tablet in the Twin Towers requests his son's name be tattooed on our nukes, right below the Nike swoosh.

5. Our nukes bow their heads, doggedly prayerful, deferential to their own enlightenment. They wait for directions from above, while globe-sized hail continues to fall, out in the great state of Texas.

6. We scope for signs of resistance from our nukes, checking for tarnishing or dulled tips indicating possible neuroticism. We get those straightened right out. We tell the good ones stories so they can sleep at night. And they dream of long dark tunnels, the brilliant, inexplicable light at the end.

COMMUNION

All day, nuns scour the *pensione*
floors with powder from a wooden
bowl. At two a.m., they lock the
stone doors. Which is how I
straddle a Roman vendor on the
back of his motorbike at 1:53,
knees gripping his hips. Roar
up my dress sleeves, camera
strap burning my neck, a strand
of beads with a cross. At
this hour, even a lean to turn
won't make me doubt how
I live, no good slip to raise
understanding like a scar. For
the dark shade has lifted from
the bird's cage, we flit through
night traffic—disco strobe now
boroughs away—and I am
urging a thief among echoes
of broken English. Cathedral-like,
the sky is a flipped bowl, bits of
cracker, accidental stars.

BEACHED

I just read in an economics book that in the history of mankind,
it's forever

been better to be a man than a woman. Perhaps this is why I
suck

at chess, why I can't get my husband's pants past my hips. I
walk the line

of blind ants, avoid ladders at night that lead to lying on roofs,
imagining

ringed planets. My grandmother's hands faintly scratched from
berry-picking,

her life an idea executed as a latticed pie. For example, me
rooted to

this couch, watching Carol Brady in bell sleeves comb fine rows
into Jan's

hair, clamping it in place with a clip. My head, too, all hair and
ears, lip-

glossed mouth blotted out. My floors, angry-clean. My acid
trips,

southerly. I lie in my life like I'm sick and it's raining. What
would it take

to scrape off the forger's pleasing copy, reveal the real pink

abstraction underneath? How much to leave the umbrella, cross
the hot

sand to set sail the raft, out where I can't touch?

AMY, WANTING A NEW SONG, IMAGINES

herself working in erotic movies—
a bad geisha girl in The Golden Fork—
her face, blank-page white, her fingertips, rubies.
She whines, the man above moves as clockwork,
drives into the black orchid wither
that lasts centuries, through white-hot crystal
meth snowfall. She zooms and bucks, hears zithers—
three-thousand-string pluck counting up total
years spent bent over in red wigs, dark edges.
Next she'll play Nicole in O.J. Gets Juiced
and each day, sours, each day, snaps, pledges
she'll quit the torn bed, the human sluice.
But then in her fist, bills. All the leaks
contained. Everything held. What Amy seeks.

BRIDE FAR AWAY

At the country club, the trees are identifiable, lush. Old enough
to make shade.

The bride steps out on the lawn for pictures and from here, her
gown is white, flounces

out from the waist in the expected way. Wind from the river
sweeps her veil a moment,

clouds her face. Dark-haired and twenty-one, she knows and
doesn't, dreams. How large

the picture in her mind. How like a stack of books—hard to hold
for long and strengthening.

All the good people will soon come from their warm and cold
rooms to watch her

shift, and her dress and train are a picture of a meadow with a
secret path. A lone man

on the river tacks his boat, leans to keep from taking on water.

PEACH DREAM

Kay is an artist and therefore dreams of moving to the country, where she can stop being a radio, a billboard, a siren. She wants to be decaying trees and vines, a hive dried of its honey. Only when inspired would she make her miniature man sculptures from colored tissue and cow dung. Kay's read books about women artists who follow heart-shaped breadcrumbs to the country, then implode inside their blue cavern skulls. She thinks of Plath, churning cherry jam, Bogan's house in flames. Whole rooms, pots of fruit, burning. Still, Kay scans the want ads for cheap acres. Her heart, locked in its smoggy pen, bleats. It is only 10 a.m. and she is hungry, imagines her plot of land with a faceless man reaching up to a peach tree. Imagines her plot of land, all the good fruit picked, with only a broken line outlining where the man had stood. 10:03. Lonely? With all her baskets brimming? None yet toppled? But each peach unsalable, carrying her tiny brand. Teeth marks in the flesh.

DEAR DARKNESS,

Nothing's coming. In childhood, all the possibly-gold daffodils were yet green bulbs, and we thrilled at shoots bumping up from dirt. Jane's now on meds, and the front lawn on Locus Lane--her old haunt--yellows, half-dead. We girls once lay there, laughing. Lara's now a star, suspended in diamond temporal planes: we can see her only in pictures. I plant tangerine pansies, try to unearth ecstasy by digging deeply. But like salt or snow, memories can sift, freeze insides. Sookie collects her sons, drives to church, runs, she has no time, she's in luck, never mulling like us over old blue stories, grasping as they try to slip away, slow hearts leaving blood on our hands. Everything alive yearns to go, but I urge too soon. The last word, a hawk's black-eyed gaze, surveying the field. How not to track movement, but listen, recall? We girls always had two wishes: to not yield. And to.

DIM INTERIOR

Back in the days I thought nothing
of filching some boyfriend, some Corey
from an orchid in dipped petals, I'd pop
as if into vaults tops from bottled beers,
lift them from cooler quarries dark—
dripping to the dare
of his driving hand. Me, in the shotgun
seat with voltage, tips of his
fingers tripping mine.
                              Months
of shoplifting the ripped fabric—itty laced
pulses—from Goods. Later sewing in my
hope chest the black pastiche heart.
                        But ripping-
off grew to big sickness—
with the frisked wrist, no longer true.
I craved tongues, strings tuned to
forlorn. Kissing that wasn't really, but
moon glue, ether.
                        Took years of
lips going drama blue till finally
the marks bitten above my black
strapless dresses. Finally looking. Down,
dandelion piles of dream, unblown.
Rapunzel tresses, shorn.

AN AMERICAN ARTIST MARRIES

But even as she gives in, promises her life this
second devotion, she keeps quiet the patch
of land covered in clover and pines
she's held onto for years.

He can't know about it exactly, just
that she often goes somewhere
days away. And when
he calls her

there, she turns to him
slowly. Her eyes
aglow, the field over-
grown in snow.

THE LETTER (1940)

where every scene contains the moon-
face of Bette Davis, damning bits of evidence:
a lace shawl, a letter, lidded eyes in the mirror.
The death-wish ivory dagger. Always the plotting
as to how one's Singapore life could turn better.
And just as dependably, the drastic misjudging.
The wrong man. She thinks she wants the one
who collects guns, the playboy in the glass-filled
haunted mansion. Schemes in her dark bungalow,
avoids her good, square husband like the sun.
Wants cigarette holders and gin, a row of linen
jackets. And vies for the playboy so hard,
shoots him dead. Listen: a woman with pickaxe
hands climbing Goldhill may need the wind cold
in her hair. But more, the fool miming stars
who loves her, who floats in a windless pond.

WEIGHING THE FIELD

The bad girls assemble again in the field of yellow-withered
shoulds.

The field is generations long and extends to a green fairy tale
woods.

There, in a hut, Snow White tucks in bedding, sings as she
works.

The good girls do. But in the field's soil, her strawberry heart
forks.

Out the window, Snow can smell tomatoes, see tow-headed
weeds

leaning. The bad girls appear as bulls—strong as their ruts are
deep,

some already with knives stuck in their spines. They nudge fat
plows,

munch stems. More blooms pop forth. The good girls croon like
cows.

On Snow's chain, a bell. She stirs warm milk, longs to become a
bull.

The bulls want to be cows: the field seems dangerously wide open,
full.

Alternate endings wait. Snow sits with her blue stockings, darning
runs.

Sits with a storm-cloud view. *Someday*, she croons, *my path will
come.*

PARTIAL PSYCHOANALYTIC TRANSCRIPT OF CHRISTMAS DAY

I'd really like to further develop the darker sides of myself, the ones different from my cousin, Doris. Like her, I've always been the good girl, smelling of pine and gingerbread, wearing a strung-lights grin, with my blond curls and candlestick figure, my skin—I'm told—tasting faintly of Jesus. What fun I'd have, surprising everyone, dressing in a black garter belt and pointed hat to toss eggs at cars. Each baked cookie winds up in someone else's throat. My hands are gift boxes. I herd the children together for church, and when they whine and plead, I tie their shoestrings too tight, feed them chocolate to keep them quiet. My husband—the fat, bearded one wearing a three-piece suit—travels to Great Britain and Europe, all across America with his job. He's been gone for the years of my red and white anger, for the thin streams of hope I swirl in like a barber shop pole. I reach out to the people I've always known, send them cheerful greetings with pictures of the children. A kind of tyranny, I know, pressing down in hopes of a response. How else do I exist? By hanging mistletoe on my door? Leaving shortbread for the mailman? One of these nights, I'll lie down in the giant outdoor crèche at the church, in the hay smelling of pigs. Curled beside the glowing Joseph, I'll sleep, till the men who determine sainthood appear again with their red gowns and rule books to lift me up to the clouds.

SIXTH GRADE DIORAMA

We slumberparty girls on the ground in Wonder
Woman sleeping bags. Stretched under
a wide black expanse of
den ceiling. All us foxes and dogs, whispering
mud, but leashed. Not yet turning for the good
lord's nudging horn, the new
girl, excluded. Father's liquor
box loomed, we little egg concoctions
would drain, re-brew. Patience having already
hitched a ride south.
Above, the fried nightlight
crucifix. Fish on a hook, wonder
bread baited. Between a chair's
spread legs, the lost pearl. The new girl's
hand in a dish of warm water? No
wonder I bit my tongue, waking
from a dream—bar
of fresh soap, fucking my mouth.

GOING BACK

The hometown you fled you can't help
but imagine as the black-eyed lover
who rose from your mussed bed
and never returned, but then changed
his mind. Now he wants you back, pines.

At eighteen, you escaped to two states
away, but only when it was clear
you'd been abandoned. You are two states
of mind: loyalty and deception. You smoke
Marlboros and drive the reddened roads at dusk.
Touch the dark mole on your chest you consider
forever excising.

Driving past the oak with scores of reaching
limbs, you find the park where you tilted
cans of beer to your lips, followed Bill or Rick
or Mike to the edge of the river to whisper
and laugh, turn serious.

The tree's roots, invisible. In breezeless air,
who heard your skirt lift. Who heard
as you imagined the trunk's insides
carved out with a clean knife.

Here's the house where someone threw
a party, and you scraped the heel of your
hand, falling beside the pool. Laughter
ricocheted off cool blue tiles. And you lay
there a moment, looking at the midnight sky
pocked with stars, shame edging like ticks
in your heart's mown paths.

And this, the house where you died
a while, breathing alone whiskey fumes
the morning you woke never more
innocently raw. The bare bulb sun never more
bald through the blinds. Where someone had
been. Had found his way in, left you
willed and undreaming. Waistband
of your jeans, hugging your feet.

Why do you come back, to the still-
hard lump where you bit off too much.
To account for years trying to chew
it down. Because the dug holes. The seeds
and roots dropped. The torn and broken-
through you long ago grew accustomed to.

Because you still need, what.

Living here was a kind of opiate
force-feeding, and the result is now
you look hard
at the two-story white houses, the deep
pools, hanging trees.

You come back, as if needing
proof of love. Aren't you something.
Standing in the shade of oaks and swaying
hope, aren't you what's left.
And enough.

WHO'S DRIVING

decides the fate of every love story, even when a cloth is sodden with wetness. He and she ride to town on a noon bus, she sitting on his handkerchief. They have been sent for groceries, he, one week new, friend to her father, under him at the Consulate. Packed in with peeling leather bags, chickens, goats, dark-eyed men speaking Spanish, not one seat bare. Bruised mango fruit, split. Sticky floor. Her blood, fed by the rules of (her father?) a different country. His heart beating, they must sit very close, a man at the front ordering all windows stay shut. Swollen clouds, his white shirt wet patched, sunned skin peeping through (him?). His arm rims their seat back, whisking her shoulders at each dip in the dirt road. Moss scent and she hears palm trees, feels green-winged birds about them, scattering (her?). The voice inside full-throated, nearly a sob. Air, thrumming with flies. Her tan skirt, it breathes if his bare leg leans. If the invisible (god?) hand—the gold chain, cross at her neck—unclasps.

POEM WITH CORSET ALLUSION

To love, Amy needs to unclench. Surrounding her, five large wooden desks, all with sharp pulls and tightly shut drawers. Impossible to budge. Her red-haired twin brothers, pockmarked and Army-issued, stuffed with defensive memos to Prom Kings and schoolyard bullies. Her sky-high, drug-happy mother, faux 18th C. tiger maple, full of hideaways for bottles of phantom cherries and rainbow pinwheel eyeballs. Her two friends, Jejune (the blond in her apartment) and Morose (the mahogany at work), taking up space, hiding return addresses in mail piles, ignoring faces heaped by the blinking red answering machine. To love, Amy needs to unclench. Demolish the desks. She has all the right gear, born with the ticking mechanisms. But the strings were cinched tight early. Cinched until her favorite color turned blue. At age twenty, she became aware she owned furniture; when she moved it around, she felt responsible. Hard to let furniture go, even the bad. Lucky for her, her mind: a room with Victorian tea rose wallpaper and loose white sheets, despite the inevitable cherry wood bed. Amy imagines someone lying. And another one lying. On the bed. And loses track of her breathing. Clench. Every day, Amy sees five hundred years into the future where all the women are like her. Very thin, withholding. The forests gone, desks everywhere. Thin-as-air women. The last generation.

THE CIRCLE

Abuse takes

Years to recognize, one

Is still inside

The reddened child sinking

In cold water
                    who looks to her adult

Arms now miming the push-

Away motion

Treading in the center
                    of the black lake, still

Trying to see through

Smoke, still trying

To get
                    why

New grass banks

On every side were sown, left

To grow, set

On fire.

GUT-ROPES
12/31/1996

She is not tired. And if she's lonely, it's only part of the story.

Night, when all is mute as a locked machine gun, the roots of her
thumbs itch in their sockets.

Winter in the night kitchen, where fig hearts in their porcelain
nest teem with the memory of winged things.

Once, she would've thrown about her arms
a shrug, gone out for beer and New Year fireworks. Now she is

half-lonely, half-knowing: rope of intuition she lights and lights
to keep from fraying. His face, lit by bright

office windows. His black-type name on white memos. Passing
him in the hall, wings.

Fused to her heart, the unsent valentine she reads in her mind.
Damp alphabet tasting of cherries,

her pulse speeds to its cursing. O, good and terrible Life, can you
bear such discreet thrill-spending?

In the night kitchen window, her lamp?

ACROSS, DOWN, BACKWARDS, DIAGONAL

love
freedom
communication
sex
safety

that heel
lean mom
hire me
his tit
why bail
we die
one

FIND-A-WORD IN MIKE AND DANICA'S MARRIAGE

S	O	W	H	O	I	S	S	H	E
S	H	E	S	N	O	B	O	D	Y
Y	O	U	R	E	A	L	I	A	R
B	I	G	S	I	L	E	N	C	E
H	E	L	L	O	H	E	L	L	O
I	M	O	U	T	A	H	E	R	E
S	O	I	S	I	T	A	M	Y	?
I	M	O	U	T	A	H	E	R	E
I	F	Y	O	U	L	E	A	V	E
Y	O	U	L	L	W	H	A	T	?

UPON LEAVING HIS WIFE FOR A YOUNG WOMAN

The sidewalk along the bridge, once wet cement.

Dara loves Adrian, stroked with a finger or stick
like an arrow.

The road, black pitch.

Below, the night river's quiver of water, no
fish. No mirror.

Weight of error, *things that were hard to bear
are sweet to remember.*

And viewed as through a reverse telescope, the
body's wet spaces.

He hears the new spark's hammer fall and fall.

Adrian loves Dara. Snow sifts down.

Tiny torn pieces of paper. Already come and

gone, the leap. Height of the journey.

NEEDS SALT

Here I stand again at the stove, stirring egg drop soup. Egg threads
rise to the top, the ladle in my fist like a riding crop. I add too much
thyme. In the distance, fire bells ring, I want to race to the burning
bank like an action hero in a plastic mask. Smell of sulphur, and I
am Patty Hearst, wanting to go where I've already been, my life
amputated again, but this time, with my own gun. Dollar signs
and question marks and hearts in a cartoon balloon beside my
head. As much as I hated it then, I want to be nineteen. When I'd
drive with windows down past his house, night jasmine wind
smelling of candy and stigmas, the line between mischief and
danger. Now I am prematurely old, swaddled in a shoebox of
gold letters. Where are my cheekbones? Parked, my truck in
the garage. Brick walk lined up like a centuries-long wall. The
soup boils, I prepare. Plain pilgrim, slicing bread. I know I am
lucky for this journey, its fleeting grace. My good man. Butter.

LOVE IS CHANGING, AND I WON'T CHANGE

I'm about to play the ingénue in a Spanish soap opera.
Tall copper-skinned black-haired Juan walks through
my trailer door to practice the kissing scene.
I dream up to the heartstopping licking of lips.
But even in the fantasy, I start coloring in the wrong
details, script curling in his fist, gold ring glinting.
Already looking for ways to flee the moment.
I get distracted not by sweatdrops on his brow or
the sound of swallowing, but the view out the
window, the horses peering from behind trailer bars,
the pupil-black of their manes, undertow of the
sun's rays. I want to be the hero. A rattlesnake curled
in the grass strikes, and I grab my rusty bike to pedal
to the vet a mile away, then return. Fiddle with the radio
till I find soothing, classical. Watch as the vet extracts
venom from the horse's leg, watch as she sews and
bundles while I talk low, make plans to buy apples.
But the dream drifts back to my window, I watch the
old blue paint rot on the trailer door. I conjure up Juan,
try to feel something.

SIXTH GRADE REDUX

At twelve, I dressed carefully. Removed from myself
even then
neckties, belts, shoestrings.

Soulfully, a wart grew at the base of my thumb,
I numbly froze it out.

As when Jennifer K's legion of lipglossers laughed,
chanted lyrics to a
Fixx song, pointed to my naked shoes.

Which I of course
took to my crew to try on a teary first-grader.

So maybe God made it happen that Always-In-Trouble
Jay opened his box of chocolate milk into my
sticker collection.

My eyes were pretty green:
I was a mean daddy sometimes a square mother.

A secret, till Mr. Are snapped a ruler and Jay spilled.

I still don't know if the red breath pulsed for Jay's taut
confession or Mr. Are's pyrotechnics.

But we tried to find out
two years after, when I spun a bottle's green mouth gently
to Jay, searching—

that first French kiss, forgiveness....

INTUITION, OR METHODS OF TRANSPORTION

Tampa's bay at night is made complete
by the airport planes flying low over it.
From your friend Isaac's stalled boat
we look up from the rippling bay
to find the lights... each time, hearing
the distant rumble before we see
the plane, which seems to amplify
somehow the boat's suggestive rocking.
Isaac tries to restart the motor, then asks
with forced lightness where your husband
Carl's work has taken him this weekend—
Philadelphia? Miami?—the southern accent
Isaac freed himself from years ago suddenly
creeping in. Salsa music from a nearby bar
fills up the space between land and water.
Little lights wink from the docks
of blacked-out houses. And the sound
of the motor catching, then the wind
from the boat's sudden skipping across water,
drown what could've been your reply.
At the next plane's roar, we look up,
and for all Isaac and I know, the plane holds
Carl, who just now might be turning
from the woman beside him, from the naked
muted interior of the plane, to gaze down
at the boats on dark, undulant water.

BRONZE MELTING

My great aunt Shea has silver hair
and papery silver hands covered in clay,
and her studio in Newark is full
of stunted figures, the smell of molten bronze.
In the kiln behind us, blurry shapes shift
and pop, and she works the clay before her,
thumbing and kneading the curves. She tells me
it will become a likeness of who she once was,
a thin red-haired woman lounging
on a bench, her hair spilling down the slats,
her mind brimming with Greenwich Village
oils, Italian men, amber-colored children.
To her, New Jersey is Moscow, all careful
strokes and snowy dim streets suggesting
Stoli, and she wears resignation like a hood
rimmed in wire. I want to ask Shea where
the sculptures of herself always disappear
to, but I don't, because she'll say,
back to the fire.

LIFE CYCLE

I. The Equal Pulls of Lust & Discipline

The woman slides her arm into burlap
and you might think this story
is about a certain sect of female Tibetan
monks and chastity: you might think
the setting, a monastery; the prop, a whip
in her hand for her back.
Yes, she is alone, but in her hand
is a potato. She withdraws it from the sack.
The burlap is camel-colored, rough
on her skin. Around her, the kitchen,
alien, the metallic appliances match the taste
on her tongue. She holds the potato,
sighs (sharp knife). She cannot move
(lucid mind). What she would do for
an orange at this moment, to peel back
its clothes, to squeeze and bite, to suck
all creation from its seeds. What she
would give to feel the sting
from its rip and kick, its defensive spit
in her eyes, everlasting.

II. Protest, Followed Eventually by Lowered Defenses

(note to former self):
You never noticed how the water,
the early dew, slid down from the pistil
(the creative center) of the lily
to its silken bottom lip, did you?
That's why I wasn't surprised
to find, for so long, a wax flower
on your lapel.

Didn't you realize flames had to surround
and waste your mind, people
had to cry, before you could find relief?
Finally, something rose up
(hope) as you let your core
be exposed. Remember
how this is done: white arms
drop their defenses as they spread
to the rain-laden sky.

III. Acceptance of Decay

Oh, mother. You told such stories
to me when I was young: men
in red velvet, on thrones. Some of them
stroking the cashmere back of the king
among beasts, all of them
with golden crowns and living in the forest.
You might have told me the forest
was a breeding ground for moss,
for green fungus and rot.
I went there to fall in love,
and I did: Decay became
what I loved most about life, the very end
of the quest for open flesh. Which was
the lion's part of the tale you forgot.

POSTCARD FROM AN OLD LOVER WITH PICTURE OF HORSE AND CARRIAGE, DRIVER AND WHIP

The rain's green forgiveness
is so much larger.
The close-mouthed snapdragons
waiting for rain.
Not so much, your postcard
in the rusted red box,
fountain pen ink blurring
characters.

You're in love with
your leaving.
Drawn hearts spilled
all about your name.

Remember the healing
salt baths? Our dry forest
scene, all sparrows feasting
on grubs and sorrow,
flying the mind's entire
distance for water. So much
smaller, that lagoon.

Pink lips of the snapdragon
open in rain.
What power, to drench!
Where I've gone, you cannot
allow.
A renegade green parrot
once enclosed.
Now in the thick wet fronds
of foreign palms.

MIXED CAMPING TRIP

Girls at eighteen have guitar
bodies. But in the middle of the
night, only a certain kind kicks
at a bonfire alone outside a ring
of tents. Up and down the long
woods, black crickets etch
blades. The rest of the world
zipped in with Army knives,
syrup, bandannas, spit.
Out of the logs, embers flip.
Cold river that goes forever
in the wrong direction. Deep
in the trees, graves, zapped
branches like arms painted
gold. The girl keeps track
without seeing: heart
intersections, picked strings.
If someone would hold her,
he could hold her back. An
owl asks. Rim of the clearing,
naked of webs and nestlings.
In the abandoned flask, what
could pass for blood.

PAINTING WITH WINTER SCENE

For fifteen years she went out wearing no
awareness. And it was then she couldn't believe
she was already dead, that nothing lay ahead
but love
she'd already tried. Unaware, she kept mixing
stranger
after stranger cocktails
of fear for her heart. Solo
flights to fish in Greenland, frozen chunks
atop bar stools. For years, raw
pink: everything strange, inviting; everything ordinary,
strange.
What to do she couldn't do: the oil painting
she carried beneath
ten protective layers,
the one of the family waiting
silent at the breakfast table as at a dark hole
in ice. Mother, father, kids in monochromatic snow,
snow, and snow.
The hands and mouths needing to be touched
up with red.

LUCKY STRIKES

You smoke those smokes and smoke
hangs between you and me, profuse obsession,
smokescreen. I'm full of no hope, I'm choking.
We've slid past sleight-of-mind tricks
to mere illusion, magic show. Now I smell
the roses, now I don't. Black cape of unchanging,
I was your lucky coin, tucked beneath a sleeve.
Talk of silver rings, intertwined, interlocked.
Then smoke, smoke, smoke, and nothing
but watching you pull a habit from a pack.
Oh, coffin nail, thin man, magician,
sawing me in half with persistence,
unwilling to quit addictions.
I begged for commitment; you yielded,
conditionally: one, two, and three days of peace,
doves released, which we have yet to know.
Someday, presto, I'll conjure a ticket—
no bags, no contraband tobacco, my heart
hidden behind scarves—and disappear into
thin air, banished by clouds of smoke,
my amateur, my pro, sweet baby of tar.

JASON LEE WHEELER'S SONG

*October, 2006: J.L.W. was given the death sentence for ambushing
and killing a Lake County deputy in the Ocala National Forest.
During the gun battle, he was paralyzed from the chest down.*

I blame my crimes on nothing but Satan,
my mom, and cocaine: all hopped up on speed
in those Ocala woods, cornered, hating
the cops and my rage, God and my need.
With a sawed-off shotgun I sprang
the good deputy—shot him in the head—
while Mama's voice chimed and cold bullets sang
(one lodged in my spine). I should be dead,
boxed up in dirt; instead, I'm paralyzed—
numb from heart down, stuck in this chair
and headed for another. I now realize
it's only dead men that crushed women bear.
I dream of trees, of limbs heavy with fruit,
though I long ago turned, sank to my roots.

MY SOUL WENT TO HASTINGS, AND ALL
I GOT WAS THIS LOUSY CRACK PIPE

At the potato chip factory in the small town
of Hastings, Florida, I get
a tour from the owner's son, Tater Lee.
Workers stand before conveyer belts,
sorting red potatoes by size: A's
this way, B's here. I say, *What's a*
normal shift? He says, *Eight to eight,*
an hour off for lunch. They used to go
till ten, with another hour off
for dinner, but they'd come back
all drunk and on crack.
He points to the horizon, across rows
to tiny homes on the edge
of the fields. *You see those? You just*
drive your car out into the middle
an wait an someone'll bring you
a vial.
It isn't long before I'm standing
at a conveyer belt, sorting. Like Vegas,
there's no clock to count minutes.
My back hurts, my hands
darken, my mind wanders. This is a good
job, better than stooping in the sun,
digging in dry ground. How gracious,
a cold beer. How long it seems I
scheme my ruby-bright plans of escape.
How much I need. Any cheap nugget
that lifts me out of here.

OCTOBER TRICKS WITH THE DENVER BRONCOS

He stands alone in his everyday baggy
fear, having heard last night the report
of neighborhood firecrackers, the Fourth
still nine months away.
Daybreak comes stiff as a
mask, his hope marching forward into
the mouth's crevasse.
                            His rituals
of desire, soaking up hours like a loaded
sponge, his trickling toward
snacks in plastic pouches —
the tagged, bagged, slightly stale bodies
of grit like dead insects, no
substance.
                        And the 2-D women in his
computer, spilling into their usual red
stretched poses, so many backlit
thorned roses. His fingers pressing
soft keys. So unlike the women
at work, their yoga class years turning
their bodies harder.
                            The air, sinking
colder.
            And he knows that it's long
past mattering that salvation will soon
arrive, as today is Sunday, and he spews
indignation toward the corner where the
confessional box sits, volume turned
low on the game.
                        Where men he can identify
will huddle close in bright orange
work clothes like prisoners.

Then steel themselves for battering.

THE NEW ART PROFESSOR, DEAD BY HIS OWN HAND

Now we've heard, we want clues: shotgun propped by a kitchen chair, bedsheet looped about an attic beam. Your students zoo about, caged. We reach out to pet them, smell the apple shampoo of their wet heads. Gray sparrows edge along limbs, sounding chip calls.

The memo announcing your death, a white tablecloth. Words lined up carefully, ready spoons. We weren't watching. Into our laps, hot soup.

Still, the air. Mound of bed, the finished corners of sheets. Fireplace, used. Ragged lawn, clipped clean. Somewhere near and far, a bowl of ash. Somewhere near and far, a cemetery.

At his desk, he's hunched above the paper ream. White sheets of long and short shadows. Taps the charcoal pencil. Too late to erase shapes he committed to. Nowhere for the pictures to go but past borders. At a certain point, how else to inhabit them fully.

ORCHID ROOM IN A BOTANTICAL GARDEN

Outside, it's twenty degrees
beneath snow-heavy clouds.
But in the greenhouse, control: closed
windows. Silent warmth, growth.
The ceiling sprays planetary mist.
Everything greens, thrives, even the cacti
soft-petaling at the root. But it's the blooms
of orchids you don't expect: geometrics
etched on red velvet, DNA loops,
hieroglyphic designs. You inhale three,
four times, nose buried to the hilt
in middles, umbilical stems, and it's natural
you feel famished, recognizing something
in the scent—pure sustenance
like bread baked next door,
even as you've never before seen orchids.
In this place, you know why it rains
on command, why nothing with a
split tongue licks the necks of orchids.
Yet how to explain your hands,
itching to pull down, to pluck, to own?

THREE RIVERS MEET, BECOME FALLS

In the documentary film about the famous architect
and his buildings, the lesser architect tries
not to sound bitter and fails; in the interview,
he describes why he's the naysayer in a chorus
of yesses for the famous one's work:
I hate to say he's overrated, but....
He sits there, buttoned up, talking high
and wounded in his throat, as though in a moment
the humidity of his pride might devolve into a river,
slip in trickles past his own pressed buttons.

Fear courses like a river as he watches himself
projected on the screen at the film's premiere,
winnows slipping like voices up his bloodstream.

His friends come round to congratulate his debut,
and in his workroom, to the only one he trusts,
he begs, I wasn't terrible, was I?
Grief nearly slips over the stones of his eyes,
a river so familiar, it goes by many names,
each source of grief named by its sufferer,
like what the architect gives his unfinished buildings.
And his friend says nothing, thinking of the many
forms of descent, of the toy-like models
on the desk behind them, each roof designed
to tilt down, to deflect rain.

HOUSE ON THE LAKE

When Dad was dying, everyone wanted
to take care of him, no one
wanted to.

We sent flowered cards, everyone wanted
the easy parts.

His cancer was a quiet purple flower
that grew too familiar when it took
over the bed.

The purple wanted the easy parts,
the purple wanted the hard parts, the liver.

We all went one way, then another.
We were the roots, we scattered.

We couldn't compete, that's all we could
do. We wanted to sit around and stare
at the clouded sky and drink.

His IV was clear, the only thing.

He had ten months, ten years.

We walked around Lily-Pad Lake,
where hordes of trout wriggled
to breathe.

We wanted to rub his feet, he didn't
want us to. He wanted a ride to the clinic,
we didn't want to go.

He did everything right, we did nothing.
We did nothing wrong, he did everything.

The flower was a new member, the kid
whose needs came first,
around whom we spoke in low tones.

Buds pressed up from under
his skin, from every conversation, dirt and
spores, torrents and sprouts.

Each day, the flower asked, What've you done
good lately?

Each morning, Dad woke at five, blinking
in the dark, thinking. He didn't want
to get up.

We all wanted to go check on him, we all
wanted to leave him alone.

He raged, dreaming. He dozed, dreaming.

Again, the air got colder and again
the Giants choked. TV from distant rooms,
Dad's cough.

We held our breath, tried to imagine.
We were nowhere close
to picking out coffins.

Each day we got closer. Someone
remembered Dad cheering Don's tennis
match, and we smiled too
wistfully.

Each day, we knew. The sun, peeping out
at the end of a dark-cloud
tunnel.

The dog jumped in the bed, disrupted
our covers.

We knew we knew nothing. We knew we did
and didn't want to be

in the dark
woods, our walls soft and yellow.

Dad, his face still
needing to be kissed:

in the woods, inside the last
house, with its yard of purple satin.

NOTES

"Kentucky Derby Poem (2008)": inspired in part by William Finnegan's article "The Countertraffickers" in *The New Yorker* (May 5, 2008).

"Poem with Bathtub, Foils": quote in section seven from Goethe's *Elective Affinities*.

"Sex Trafficker's Pantoum": first and final line borrowed from Mr. Finnegan's article.

"How to Pick a Lock": quotes and ideas borrowed from *Ted the Tool's MIT Guide to Lock Picking*.

"Our Nukes": inspired in part by Steven Okazaki's documentary, *White Light/Black Rain: The Destruction of Hiroshima and Nagasaki*.

"Upon Leaving His Wife for a Young Woman": quote from Roman philosopher Seneca the Younger (1 BC-AD 65).

"Three Rivers Meet, Become Falls": inspired by Sydney Pollack's documentary, *Sketches of Frank Gehry*.